The Harry Hanukkah Storybook

Written by:
Jazan Wild

Artwork by:
Iwan Nazif

Colors by:
Yuan Cakra

Editing by:
Sharon Levesque Barnes

A Production of Carnival Comics®.

One snowy day, while playing, Nicholas heard an odd sound coming out of the woods near the orphanage.

Despite a blizzard and Ms. Epoh's calls, he followed the echoes of a baby crying, deep into the forest.

Nicholas was led to a mysterious candlelit cave where a baby boy with a dreidel in hand, lay under a Menorah.

Nicholas brought the** happy **little bundle of joy back to the orphanage where all the children eagerly awaited.

Ms. Epoh held the baby as Nicholas guessed his name. "*Ha--y Hannukah*? It must be *Harry Hannukah*! See?"

"Thicker than blood, tougher than skin, family is who you love, it's who you let in." They became brothers.

One blustery day, while stuck inside, bored and toyless, the children gave Nicholas a wonderfully brilliant idea.

Nicholas began to sneak out back to the old woodshed behind the orphanage and secretly make toys.

The morning that followed the *Night of Giving* found all the orphaned children waking up to toy-filled stockings.

Word spread of a mysterious toymaker granting children's wishes. And so, many more wishes came.

The *Winter Wind* knew exactly who the secret toymaker was, and soon so did Harry. "I knew it was you!"

Harry promised to keep Nicholas' secret. Better yet, he decided that he wanted to help build toys, too.

But there were just too many wishes to fulfill.
They needed some magic... and so some magic came.

Ewald and his merry band of elves built toys all through the night to make sure all would be ready for the big day.

The toymakers awoke to find every letter fulfilled, yet they still had no way to deliver the gifts to town. Until...

...the elves showed up! And by magical means, they tossed all the many toys into one enchanted velvet sack.

Nicholas picked up the sack and each elf gasped in awe. They now had their sleigh driver and so much more.

The elves now had a driver, but who'd pull their sleigh? Ewald whistled and eight reindeer answered the call.

The elder elf sprinkled about some magic dust and when it settled, the enchanted garb had found its toymaker.

"Now Dasher, now Dancer, now Prancer and Vixen! On Comet, on Cupid, on Dunder and Blixem!" said Nicholas.

At the first stop Nicholas and the elves leapt to the roof. With a touch to the nose, down the chimney they went.

Annabelle wished only for a doll for her sister; moved by her letter, Nicholas brought a doll for each girl, instead.

Dear Toymaker,

My Mommy and Daddy have worked very hard this year, but there is not enough money for toys for me and my sister.

I'm not asking for anything for myself, however, if you could bring my little sister a toy that would be wonderful.

You truly are The Winter Saint.

Warmly, Annabelle

At the end of the night, a mystical snow globe showed Harry, that Isaak, had written him a truly sad letter.

Dear Toymaker,

Please don't forget about me when you deliver your toys. I heard some other children say you're going to bring them toys on the Night of Giving.

But then they began to laugh at me and said no one was going to bring me any toys because I'm different... because my family celebrates a Festival of Lights.

They told me it was weird and so was I. It made me sad. So, I cried, just a little. Then I thought, magic doesn't make you cry.

So I'm writing you anyway.

Please visit our house, if you can. And yes, I believe in you.

Your friend, Isaak.

"Turn the sleigh around! We have one more run to make before dawn!" cried out Harry, and off they went.

The sleigh was led to a house with a candlelit window. Harry left a note and the spinner he'd had his entire life.

Harry knocked, then ran off, as to not be spotted; and just in time, as Isaak opened the door with heart racing.

Dear Isaak,

I'm Nick the Toymaker's friend. I also make toys in my friend's workshop. I read your letter.

By way of magic, it led me to you tonight... to the candle in your window. I was told it once burned bright for eight days in a row when darkness desperately tried to set in.

That's why there are eight candles. What most people don't know... is that the ninth candle in the middle, which burns brightest... that one is you!

Your friend,

Harry Hanukkah.

The boys who'd picked on Isaak, now were wowed by the gifts; all except Rudiger, of course. "My bike is better."

Word of the candlelight gift-giver, Harry Hanukkah, began to spread from town to town, village to village.

Amongst all the happiness, Nicholas had to tell Harry a secret... that he'd be leaving the orphanage soon.

Just a day after their great run, more letters began to arrive, only now, they had Harry's name on them, too.

The day Nicholas spoke of arrived; his 18th birthday. Harry was very sad to see him go, and so was Ms. Epoh.

Instantly, more letters for Harry arrived, but before he could grab them, the wishes blew away into the forest.

Harry chased the letters to the same candlelit cave he'd been found in. Inside was a magical suit of his very own.

Now suited up, Harry jingled the bells upon the tip of his hat and at lightning speed returned to the orphanage.

As the months passed by, Harry worked tirelessly in the old woodshed, all the while, awaiting the return of...

...“Nicholas!” And the *Night of Giving*, of course. Harry had a surprise of his own; a new blue suit, bells and all!

Magic dust sprinkled over silver bells made the reindeer fly, so Nicholas decided to give landing on roofs a try.

**Harry jangled the bells on the tip of his hat, and said,
"I'll meet you at the edge of the village, in no time flat!"**

The two toymakers had many more runs, until Harry's 18th birthday, when the sleigh carried him away, too.

Over the* North Pole*, the storm gave way to a snow globe-like dome, which magically opened for the sleigh.

Once inside the dome, Nicholas showed Harry all around Santa's Village. On the other side of Main Street was...

...Harry's new home, *Hanukkah Hallow!* Within *Hanukkah Hall* were Mendel and the rest of the workshop gnomes.

In the many *Night of Givings* that followed, the two toymakers' generosity became known around the world.

Season after season was full of joy, until one day when a small crack appeared right in the middle of Main Street.

Harry's globe revealed the reason for the sudden divide... it was caused by angry voices carried on the *Winter Wind*.

The foul wind even caused a rift between the elves and gnomes over cargo space, until their bosses stepped in.

When the *Night of Giving* arrived, the sleigh just made it into the air. Now, the crack ran down *all* of *Main Street*.

That night, at the end of their run, just before sunrise, angry voices from the village below, began to ring out.

Best friends, Benjamin and Jacob, gave each other gifts, however, their fathers got mad over differing beliefs.

When Benjamin pleaded for everyone to stop fighting, the *Winter Wind* heard his plea and sent two toymakers.

The spiraling gust had something to say, too, so he took human form and approached the quarreling fathers.

The *Winter Wind* showed the entire village how these two orphans from different worlds, became family.

"I carry all of your emotions, so choose joy, just as these magical toymakers did," said the *Winter Wind*, parting.

Harry Hanukkah **and** ***Nicholas Kristoff Kringle*** **gave each of the fathers, the very gifts they'd wished for long ago.**

“Here, Jacob, for you and your friend,” said Mr. Kopel.
He turned to thank the Toymakers, but they were gone.

Jessica, Hailey, and all the citizens of the *North Pole*, cheered as the sleigh landed upon a restored *Main Street*.

Each year, the toymakers embark on another sleigh ride. "Race you to the edge of town! Merry Chrismukkah!"

One girl who knows who won the race that night, almost didn't. See, after being teased, she threw away her wish.

"A menorah is magical, so why can't I believe in Harry Hanukkah?" thought Rachel, and quickly grabbed a pen.

Dear Harry Hanukkah,

I am sorry for writing to you
so late this year. But it took a little
bit of time to figure out just what
I wanted to ask for.

And after giving it much thought,
I have decided that the thing that
I would wish for most is for many
more Happy Hanukkahs, and
many more visits from you,
Harry Hanukkah.

The best gift you ever gave me,
were the memories.

Love, Rachel

P.S. I still do believe.

When Rachel went to get a stamp, an enchanted gust swept her letter away, through the smallest of cracks.

Rachel chased after the letter, but it rose like a kite. Crushed, she fought back tears; then a ring and a knock!

Rachel heard bells as she opened the door and that's when she saw him, Harry Hanukkah! He left her a note.

To Rachel,

Ring these, whenever you need
to awaken the magic within.

Your friend,
Harry Hanukkah

P.S. Sorry for the short reply,
but I gotta run. I'm racing Nicholas
to the edge of town and I'm winning.
A secret... the milk and cookies
always slow him down.

The next morning
Rachel's letter was on the front page
of newspapers around the globe!

After the story of the letter hit the press,
a Harry Hanukkah song that tells the tale
of the notorious Toymaker's adventures,
climbed to the top of the Holiday Charts!

To think that this wonderful tale all began
with two orphans who found each other
long ago and decided to make the
world a better place.

As the Toymakers would often say...
"Thicker than blood, tougher than skin,
family is who you love, it's who you let in."

Harry and Nicholas decided to let in
children's wishes throughout the world.
That being said, this all beckons
one magical question...

"Do you believe?"

The End.

North Pole News

December 26th Breaking News

HARRY HANUKKAH SPOTTED!

A CHRISMUKKAH MIRACLE!

Christmas and Hanukkah coincided with one another this year. It has long been said that this is a magical occurrence, indeed. As of the time of this printing, there have been numerous sightings of Santa Claus and Harry Hanukkah, with several elves and gnomes riding upon a sleigh, traveling at near supersonic speeds.

While most have been overjoyed, there are some complaints rolling in, as well. Some are saying that their windows have been shaken as the so-called sleigh flies overhead. Still others have complained of hearing a loud ringing sound, not unlike that of silver bells, which they say, woke sleeping children and pets alike.

ONE LITTLE GIRL'S STORY SAYS IT ALL!

"I HEARD HIS BELLS AND EVEN GLIMPSED A SIGHT!"

However, one sighting that stands out from the crowd is a young girl who chooses to remain anonymous. What makes her tale different than the rest is the fact that she has a handwritten letter, by none other than, Harry Hanukkah, himself.

Several authenticators seem to suggest that when the handwriting samples were tested against Issak Eisen's Harry Hanukkah letter, the initial findings point towards... a match. Even though, the letters were written hundreds of years apart.

Authentic? The real deal? You decide.

THE HARRY HANUKKAH SONG

CARNIVAL MUSIC SERIES

PRESENTS:

THE HARRY HANUKKAH SONG / APP-D SINGLE

www.jazanwild.com/HARRYHANUKKAH.mp4

BONUS ARTWORK

(IMAGES FROM THE HARRY HANUKKAH STORY)

BONUS ARTWORK

(IMAGES FROM THE HARRY HANUKKAH STORY)

BONUS ARTWORK

(IMAGES FROM THE HARRY HANUKKAH STORY)

BONUS ARTWORK

(IMAGES FROM THE HARRY HANUKKAH STORY)

BONUS ARTWORK

(Images From The Harry Hanukkah Story)

BONUS ARTWORK

(IMAGES FROM THE HARRY HANUKKAH STORY)

Made in the USA
Monee, IL
04 October 2025